SOMEONE TELL US WHERE WE'RE GOING

Poets Wanted Anthology
2020

Copyright © 2020 by Falkenberg Press. All rights reserved. No portion of this book, except for review, may be reproduced, stored in a retrieval system, or transmitted in any form or by any means—electronic, mechanical, photocopying, recording, or otherwise—without written permission of the publisher.

ISBN 978-1-953868-00-8

First edition November 2020

Published by
Falkenberg Press
Berkeley, CA

Cover art and design by Audrey Mei

TABLE OF CONTENTS

About Poets Wanted

Note from the Publisher

AWAY

Gary Dalen	Endless Summer	11
Dee diSomma	Moonrise	12
Keith Mark Gaboury	Based on a True Story	14
Doug Young	Fly Basic Steerage!	17
Kazue Watanabe	The Fault of Uber	19

HERE

Keith Mark Gaboury	I Left My North Oakland Shadow	22
Kazue Watanabe	24Th Street, Mission, San Francisco	25
Leena Prasad	tanka	26
Dee diSomma	grey sky day	27
Doug Young	Wandering About, in Berkeley	29
Ana Delgadillo	Monday	30

MIRAGE

Phoenix Gilliam	Peaking	35
Gary Dalen	guru	37
Leena Prasad	Facebook	39
Audrey Mei	Radio Boy	40
Keith Mark Gaboury	Tongue Swapping 1	42
Ana Delgadillo	Ocean & Layers	44
Kazue Watanabe	White Cat	51

WITH YOU

Phoenix Gilliam	If I were a dream	54
Dee diSomma	dawn joy – October 6, 1975	56
	dawn joy, redux - August 26, 2015	
Gary Dalen	Timid Romantic	59
Audrey Mei	If I am breathing	61
Keith Mark Gaboury	Tongue Swapping 2	63
Ana Delgadillo	Message from Time to Clock	64

ROUND TRIP

Leena Prasad	time	68
Frances Hillyard	I see you among yellow roses	69
Dee diSomma	A long and lonely vigil	71
Phoenix Gilliam	Two Survivors	72
Ana Delgadillo	Río Papaloapan	74

EXPRESS WAYS

Audrey Mei	orgies of the electrical poets	78
Gary Dalen	Recipe for a painter	80
Leena Prasad	unpoetic	81
Dee diSomma	the soft hiss of pencil on paper	82

THE POETS   84

About Poets Wanted

I am a poet.

I no longer feel an internal kick of doubt when I utter these words because Poets Wanted, a poetry group I founded, enabled me to gain this assurance.

Poets Wanted meets once a month. We bring copies of poems we have written, listen to them read out loud, and hold our breath as people tell us what we crafted well and what can be further fine-tuned.

These monthly meetings nourish my relationship with poetry. Although a free-verse poet for most of life, I wrote haiku as Twitter updates during National Poetry Month and collected these into a book *not exactly haiku*. I am invited to author talks due to my book and sell copies at events. In 2017, a poem I wrote was published in an anthology, *Sonoma: Stories of a Region and Its People*. By then, Poets Wanted had been marching along for over a decade. I still did not feel that I could call myself a poet.

In 2018, a friend invited me to read haiku from *not exactly haiku* at a meeting of her writing group. Expecting a small gathering, I was surprised to see over a dozen people tightly assembled at a cramped table in a small cafe in Hayward, CA. Introduced as the "guest author," I read a few haiku. I was shocked when six people purchased my book. Usually, I'm lucky if I sell one copy at formal author events. Before that day, people had introduced me as a poet, I was asked by the California Writers Association to create and host a poetry writing group, and someone even recited one of my haiku at a gathering. Somehow, that day in a small Hayward cafe tied all the knots together and, as I rode home on BART, I started thinking of myself as a poet.

The confirmation came again when my experiment with tanka resulted in positive feedback. I ventured into limericks and made people laugh with some of my work. I was able to spin out tankas and limericks as if poetry was a language in which I had gained some fluency.

The evidence was starting to build and today I can say "I am a poet" with only a tiny hiccup of doubt. Poets Wanted helped fuel my poetry ventures and inspired this anthology.

A few years ago, I moved the group from its San Francisco location to Berkeley. My friend Audrey Mei lives in Berkeley and started to attend the poetry workshops. The idea for an anthology sparked during a Poets Wanted meeting and Audrey volunteered to be the publisher.

All the contributing poets are members of Poets Wanted. Join us if you are a poet, even if you are not ready to say that you are. Details about the monthly meetings are available at: PoetsWanted.com.

Leena Prasad

Note from the Publisher

Imagine the clatter of dishes and the din of student conversations echoing off the wood and mirrors at Au Coquelet Café in Berkeley. They were bright Sunday afternoons when Poets Wanted convened monthly for years. That reality, of course, has unexpectedly slid into the distant past.

I chose the title for this anthology at the very beginning of 2020, before the world shut down. Because even without a pandemic, poets often feel lost, floating in a limbo between emotions, insecurity, and purpose, all while asking themselves the impossible questions: Is this poem done? Am I wasting my time? Will anyone want to read this?

And of course: Where is this going? For poets, the unknown can generate a storm of creativity, yet each time we're unsure if its winds will carry us or drop us in the middle of a field. We rarely have control. And now, the entire world has lost control, things that were never supposed to move have crumbled away. But also, it's a chance for any person to dip into the poet's mind, to experience an uncertainty so everlasting that a poet has no choice but to marry it.

This set of poems was published not as a contest, but as an expression of a tiny local group of poets. As a genuine cross section of our community, a snapshot of the Bay Area under its skin. We hope to share with you the dynamic moment when poets casually come together around the table, listen, talk a little, and then go their own ways.

Audrey Mei

AWAY

GARY DALEN

Endless Summer

By chance if I make a mistake,
    I won't forgive you.
By virtue if I create a law,
    you can arrest me.
By authority if I read a poem,
    you can have it.
By religion I can poison your wine,
    so you can actually enjoy the taste.
By revolution things change,
    so there is a reason to change them back.
By art I can lie in bed with any woman I want,
    as long as she wants to lie in bed with me.
By luck we fall in love with things,
    unless you play the horses.
By education things become misread,
    because they are re-read.
By culture we are imprisoned in freedom,
    even if a door is left unlocked.
By experience a young boy can look up a lady's dress
    and not be noticed.
By reason absurdity is accepted,
    as long as it rhymes with logic.
By seeking we find different truths,
    that give us reason to argue, fight,
    and sometimes kill.
By wisdom we become enlightened,
    to the realization that we know nothing.
By love everybody stinks,
    sexual organs disintegrate,
    bones turn into ashes,
    and whatever remains becomes
    an endless summer.

Moonrise

The wind sighs through the sage.
A few birds sing their evening song.

In the east, the sky is a deep blue,
To the west, a fringe of fire clings, beyond the mountains.

The day gives way to night,
And the magic of the desert awakens.

Night birds claim the lower sky
In their search for food.

A conundrum: life begets
life in its own death.

Stars grow bright.
To the east, anticipation.

A cool light slowly rises and grows
Until the moon appears, veiled in thin clouds

The stillness grows,
All beings pause at the power of moonrise.

Quiet flows,
As moonlight spreads across the sage.

These moments,
Filled with a power beyond the touch of man,

A celebration of life,
A moment in eternity.

Based on a True Story

In the beginning, Eve stood in a garden's blueprint sunlight. She picked a red globe from a thoughtful branch. After she bit into that trespassing delight, Adam tore his teeth into the southern hemisphere.

A chunk happily lodged itself behind his Adam's apple. Eve peered down his blocked tunnel when the fruit barked *Fuck Off*. This was of course the first *Fuck* spoken in the history of humankind.

Before she would pass on this verbal whip to her children, they exited the garden to the hospital run by the neighborhood squirrels and rabbits. Within a sapling grove, Adam jammed a stick down his throat to puncture a breathing hole. On a waiting room log, he bantered with a beaver mother whose son's tail got ripped off by a bear.

Up at the front desk of sculpted timber, Eve's red eyes pleaded with a squirrel receptionist who consumed her gaze on collecting and scooping up acorns into a tight fist over to the breakroom. Once she scurried back, Eve dolloped tree wax onto the receptionist's tongue and slapped on a customer dissatisfaction survey.

When she found Adam collapsed in mud, his blue-sky face staring up at a shrugging sky, she pushed him over the counter where they found Dr. Furry Rabbit smoking in a blooming shadow.

Hey are you the new bipeds everyone's talking about?
Yes and this apple won't let Adam breathe.
Well have you tried fire?

The doctor tossed his lit smoke inside, which scorched the blockage before rushing down to flame lick his red heart black.

As Eve burrowed her head inside to spit out the destruction, she remembered she came out flush from the Earth with two hearts. With a quarter lung co-pay signed off in blood, Dr. Furry Rabbit finished the surgery in a virgin dusk.

Two beats shambled back to the soil of our genesis, but they could not return to the garden. Its gate was locked and bark burned to the ground.

DOUG YOUNG

Fly Basic Steerage!

*Announcing an Exciting New Class as Our
Punishment for Cheap Losers*

Excited we announce today
For low class flyers, keep at bay
The Spirit of our enemy
Our friendly skies make discount free

For thrifty losers, Steerage Class!
Titanic, lifeboats, die alas
It's your damn fault we can't compete
Who clicks to buy the lowest seat

So cause regret and punish them
Make arbitrary rules for when
No online check-in, boarding pass
Waste hours in line, you cheap dumb ass

Scum liars claim no carry-on
Inspect and measure, prove them wrong
Associates who won't enforce
Will lose their jobs forthwith due course

We'll drag them from their seats for fun
In Steerage there's nowhere to run
Corporate anger, mal intent
Harsh rules for dimwits, vile contempt

We hate them with a passion fueled
Lost gate slots, family jewels
Define class Basic, pain, chagrin
Locked in steerage, next of kin

KAZUE WATANABE

The Fault of Uber

6pm Friday evening
Bus 22 stuck in traffic
A man sitting behind me furious
on the phone he repeats

I will never make it on time
It's because of this traffic
Uber cars everywhere

I prepared everything for this day
Sleepless nights and no weekends
And I will never make it on time
Because of Uber cars

A vibrant Friday evening on bus 22
fire alarms and house music outside
5 people on the bus
Quietly sitting

I want to bomb Uber cars
I will never make it on time
Uber cars everywhere
And destroying our lives

There is no sound on the bus
Other than this man's rant
The bus moves slowly
Arriving at Mission and 16th stop

HERE

I Left My North Oakland Shadow

In the oxygen bath
of Ocean Beach, a smirking wind
slapped me back on my ass

where my heart
slunk out onto sand.
She slimed away

towards a rose garden
before the Dutch Windmill's
ancient blades.

I walked east
to grab a hunk
of Alamo Square grass.

Roots in hand, I flipped my finger
at the native glory
of the Painted Ladies' sheen.

Did I scandalize
the four postcard temples?
A fanny pack tourist chuckled,

his money legs sprinting over
for a selfie with my dead eyes
but I pushed him into a gutter.

I needed to find my heart
lost somewhere in a grid
I couldn't grapple. At last, I spotted her

sobbing on Panhandle concrete,
a rose petal on her lips, she exclaimed
I saved some nectar for you.

I smiled and stuffed her
behind my ribs:
she snuggled oh so warm
like a slug after a morning storm.

KAZUE WATANABE

24TH STREET, MISSION, SAN FRANCISCO

You walk down east on the 24th street from 24th and Mission Bart station. You see a tree-lined street that might remind you of somewhere else. Maybe somewhere in South America. Maybe somewhere in Spain. Somewhere anonymous, somewhere far away, but still somewhere familiar. Away from the chaos of hip mission, away from the usual chill and fog of San Francisco, away from the shiny stores and restaurants, this sunny corner of the city, a still unknown favorite secluded for the locals, is an oasis, to those of us who want to hide, who want to acquire solitude at no cost.

Now the year is 2018, and of course the scene has changed. You walk down the street and see a new ice cream joint that looks like a brand-new tiled bathroom, in between two old taquerias. Then two other taquerias and a nice old adobe bookstore continue. You tell yourself probably you were seeing illusions of some sort. But when you start to forget that you think you saw a yuppy business on the street, you suddenly see a wine bar that serves $13-a-glass wine. The further you walk the rest of the street, their number increases. Gradually you start to feel like you're starring in a zombie flick. The character encounters one zombie, and then another one when you almost forgot about it, then the number starts to multiple as the time goes by.

Probably this is the time you start to ask the question. Is it the street that has changed? Or is it you that has changed. Is it the scenery that's all to be blamed? Probably that's not true. Maybe it's you who is a zombie, lamenting on the never-changing Mission that only existed in your head, nurtured by the imaginary fish taco, and not by $5-a-cup lavender vanilla ice cream, which is becoming more real than ever.

tanka

the plan is to write
on, a tanka 5-7-5-7-7
with a 2-line twist
yet here I am, simply
writing some nonsense

DEE DISOMMA

grey sky day

A thin rain soaks into the parched hills,
    the first winter rain.
The misty hills become walls,
    the wet sky a ceiling,
As I wander through eucalyptus and bay.

The chill in the air
    awakens my senses.
Rainy-sky days are
    days of contemplation,
Aimlessly wandering within
    as my feet carry me over the hills.

The wilderness calls to me again,
    and I long to run free in the hills.
But I cannot run forever;
    I must rest at times.
Standing under a dripping tree,
    I watch sheets of rain chase through the air.

The rain wraps a cool grey cloak about me,
    sheltering me from distraction.
The hills show my feet a path to tread,
    leading nowhere special.
In my mind, I will rediscover
    the person who lives inside me

We have been strangers too long.

Wandering About, in Berkeley

Robbed in Gourmet Ghetto, normally safe.
I was out late, my fault, seeking love.
Punched kicked, Spruce home limped, emasculated.
Covid-snapped so got Zoom zapped, pity me.

Next morning skateboarding, glory, my luck changed.
On Shattuck, crashed hydrant - no, it's a GIRL!
Her face in blood, couldn't see, was she cute?
Turns out she's tall, not so stout, lucky me!

Paul ... She has a boyfriend? ... helped her. I'm bummed!
But wait, Paul's fly hat and waders I recognize
And is not stout tall girl's vest also mine?
They wear my gear Paul stole from me, the swine!

Policeman licks pastry from fingers between
Rose and Vine – should I shout, turn Paul in?
To get back my hat? No! To get rid of him!
If I don't, he'll camp on her like glue.

I can't let her know it was me run Paul through
There'd be no tall not stout girl that way too.
I'd be wandering about still late at night
For love, pray tell, what's my best move?

Monday

4:45
My first alarm goes off, like a small flame it takes me into its arms but I swat at it to quiet.

5:05
Snooze is no one's friend.

5:30
JT blasts close to my ears, the rattling of bones as he promises parties, my body lays dead beneath the blanket.

6:10
You know that time when a hammer hits the nail, when the nail finds itself stuck on the badly painted wall? When rigidity is only a clue of how you'd wish to stay but can't. Traffic building a pyramid of red lights that slowly I must climb.

6:45
I almost hit a turkey, or maybe it wanted to be hit by me.

7:20
Spaces are made to be backed into, sometimes the only row comes in the backwardness of tail lights, in the knowledge that you've arrived and the day is not over.

8:00
The empty minds of youth walk in to be filled, but never entertained.

12:30
I eat the thought of food, the taste of half a day. They say to look at life as half full, the glass never empties and the hours pour on like saliva in the craving.

3:00
Outside parents gather like honking geese that won't disperse. They connect in formations blocking my way out, my escape, my hope for serenity in the loudness of blowing horns.

I almost hit a kid, jaywalking, the crosswalk ten feet away. He looks at me and laughs as the music digs into his eardrums, as the day empties in each step like sweat across his brow. I think he was one of mine once, sitting in the corner, his book a folded pillow that spoke to him in Spanish, too bad English was never his best subject.

4:00
I sit, breathe in the smells of cars that stop and go like turtles. A man's cigar lights its way past the dry coughs of car exhausts. He sings at the top of his lungs a Drake song that doesn't fit white fingers, the closest is the reddish tan of sun from rolled up sleeves.

There is no space in front of me, and time has already pushed past me like flies going to die.

5:30
Destination reached.

6:00
Fingers tap the remnants of the day, the breaking of youth lost, empty seashells the ocean has left behind. I wonder away to a world that is not mine, to swim amongst the seaweed wrapped grains of rice that sink in the rich darkness of soy sauce.

9:00
Sleep feathers best when undone in the cool breeze of the fan, as it touches me, the rustles of the sheets against my skin.

I know day will wake me, but until then I belong to the silence of the night.

MIRAGE

Peaking

Love is an allowance.
Reach the sky and pull down handfuls of heaven.
I am the nature of my own becoming,
registered with the motives of creation.
This thickening night
forest of forever
enlifted with beginnings.
Skyward the blossoming arrows.
Fountainings of arrival
draw the fortune of angels

guru

While on the spiritual path, waiting for the sun to rise, came about an institutionalized nut, eating a saltine cracker, sitting inside, resting his mind. Waiting to say goodbye, he spoke of alien beings as not being free, for they had peeked at him while hovering above the overcast sky. Falling leaves never lie, truth is in the quiet breeze. He thought, was he a teacher? He went on to tell him how sour hatred spills off the decks of ships as they journey through the dark night of the soul, rounding the horn. Be on your way, and when you wake up, don't forget to feed the hungry children if you want to live.

An endless goodbye to love, manifesting stress inward and outward, throughout the whole nasty world. Hope becomes a poem, lust becomes survival. Knowledge piles up its garbage, in the sacred foundation of narcissistic love.

She followed him into the cafe, she followed him into the movies, but she did not follow him home. For home does not exist, not for him or anyone else. It is only an illusion, a place to hide from love, to shelter the ego, to unbind, to disunify, to pray for war. Yes, she did not follow him home, the beautiful being she was, who triggered his imagination, his life blood. He had hoped to make passionate love to her and discuss poetic inspiration and opposing contraries such as hate and love, sweet and sour.

Facebook

people's lives, thoughts
arranged for my consumption
within the Facebook frames –
my time withdrawn for this
but is it with interest or loss?

Radio Boy

Lights streak past the window
I sip my psychedelic tea.
In a beating plume canary blue
You are huddled next to me.

The speaker heads are throbbing
There's a party on this train.
Shimmy close together kids,
it's not the same blame game.

Hear the glasses clinking?
It's the dancing Radio Boy.
In the field he's a twirling,
swirling baby wooden toy.

The Chinaman's in the corner
with his arms folded crossed.
One day he is sexy,
Another day he's not.

And the Captain's up in front
with the headphones on.
He tapped that jumpin' pedal
and Whoooosh! We was gone!

The trumpet blows my hair off
Pushing time as fast as it can.
Look, the dancing Radio Boy
Is now a Radio Man.

But wait a moment, sir,
It seems there's something wrong.
We think we ran a traffic light
And lost our lovin' song.

"Be still kids!" yells the Captain.
"You can help me find the beat
Point your nose up in the air
And keep your bottom on the seat."

"See those crazy circles
in the pulsing auburn sky?
Follow the signal up the hill!
There's a tower rising high!"

We see it in the distance
Yes, the epicenter's hot!
Atop the metal cross beams
There's the tiny burning spot.

Are you sure that's what we want, sir
since we do not have a home?
We've been traveling for ages
We don't want to be alone!

"This time I know it's right.
It's the wise wind blowin'."

Well, we hope you know where we're going, sir
We hope you know where we're going.

Tongue Swapping 1

Sally stole my poet tongue last night
while I dreamed
about an uprising of tongues.

When I awoke
to a gaping wound, she meowed
I already swapped yours
with Lenny the Lion.

After Sally sewed my ferocity in,
she led the way to the bodega
on E. 4th & Avenue C

where Simon greeted us
behind the domain of his counter.
Did you hear? We're selling
lion's milk now.

Once I groomed myself
with my sandpaper tongue,
I grabbed a quart
of interspecies delight.

South to Houston honking,
we sprinted down a F bus.
As I panted in this transit squeeze,
a businessman stepped

onto my wild identity
drooping onto the black floor.
Naturally I growled

with an unfurled anger
into his cubicle eyes.
He cowered behind a blind woman

and I chugged back my quart
on that bus bumping over potholes to
The Central Park Zoo.

Ah yes, a new exhibit
spotlights Lenny the Lion.
We shamble up to his cage

to offer our milk
as he recites *Leaves of Grass*
from a diorama of fake nature.

Ocean

1. Sunlight

I drift within
waves smaller
than those that sift
   for ghosts
along the beach.
Water wakes
the shell that makes
up my body,
   my toes
       reach
   for Twilight
as tiny fish dart through
leaving scratches
along my skin.
My fingers
   stretch,
       touch
the grey fiberglass hull,
I watch the *Mona Lisa's*
sails spread like my hair
against my shoulders
as I push away.

2. *Twilight*

Eyes close,
my arms wrap,
I dissipate,
salt
    mixes
        with salt,
my soul seeps through
my toes to where the sun
is just a ghostly light
surrounded by jellyfish
lamps that catch
    falling
        marine snow,
an oarfish swims upwards,
its body a luminescent harp
only the ocean can play,
I dive towards midnight.

3. Midnight

Ghost ships sleep
amongst the flickers
of luminescent creatures
that have yet to be named,
I pass through a dark
canvas as fish swim by
leaving light
imprinted
    lithographs
that point me
to hunt for the abyss.

4. The Abyss

Pressure,
    my ears
           implode
   into darkness
I will only know
   in life,
but have no room
for it here.
I
   drown
           deeper.

5. The Trenches

Tectonic plates
dive
    one
        under
        another.
Cerberus waits
  in the shadows,
but I am not
    Persephone.
The depths
    of my being
        Metamorph
            in the dark.

Layers

I search for sunlight
in the ocean's depths,
a depressive pressure
    tightens
around misread diagnoses.

Notes,
reminders of darkness
swallowing,
    flushing pill
        by pill,
with a promise of light,
where it has failed to enter.

I am shipwrecked
beneath its sludge,
the only waves a mirage
    of dirty waters.

At times twilight depths lift,
a manic impulse floats
    outside
        midnight,
a rising wind drives
my tangled sails forward
    directionless,
my actions bitterly sting,
salt against my face.

I've made myself a tribe
but one
   by one
         they drown,
get lost,
   leave me
         to feast alone.

Yet I turn,
        turn
   in my darkest times
the moon's reflection
on the surface,

   I roam
through wreckage left behind,
search for a way
     back
         to sunlight.
Far off I hear *Abuelo's* voice mumbled
as if through a water bubble.

"Do not search within
        the trenches,
enfócate en las etapas
       que la vida surge en tí,
but in the layers
   that life
      surfaces within
         YOU."

It is difficult to stop
            to search
                        to focus
                                    to know
the steps
            I've taken.

How do I decipher
    layers
            given
                        to me,
to know a place
safe in the wrinkles
            of my hands.
Like waves find land
            and never stay
                        I am not
                                    done changing.

KAZUE WATANABE

White cat

There is a white cat on the sidewalk of 17th and de Haro
on the front step of the building that used to give
    dance classes in the evenings
around the corner a new laundry and tailor service opened up
two blocks away there is a new whole foods building

There is a white cat on the sidewalk of 17th and de Haro
he is usually by himself but sometimes he has a guest,
    another cat, rather orange not white
he is usually making a bed, or already curled up and asleep,
    but sometimes he paints
to my surprise he has a whole painting kit, oil colors and brush
also i catch him sometimes reading
i want to ask what he reads but i never have enough courage

There is a white cat on the sidewalk of 17th and de Haro
right in front of the bus stop where muni 22 stops
around 6 pm young programmers working in the neighborhood
    gather around, waiting for a bus
they chat about their hometowns, about old friends,
    new apartments and jobs
they and the white cat are invisible to each other

There is a white cat on the sidewalk of 17th and de Haro
he never looks hungry nor unhappy
curled up reading his books

WITH YOU

If I were a dream
and you were a dreamer
could I hold you while you sleep
and just beyond the sorrow
touch the secrets that you keep

The ones you said you'd only tell
a lover while you lay
beneath him like a summer
as the daylight slips away

You'd plant Dahlias and lavender
beneath the nurturing showers
but you're not a summer and I'm not a dream
and you only wanted stolen flowers

Your breast a haunted battlefield
Shiva destroyer's sails becalmed
charnel smoke behind your eyes
your face a softly spoken psalm

Your soul, to me, a phantom ship
on a foggy, barren shore
and the feral rush of nature
to the vacuum she abhors

We took more from love than what was ours
You and I were born to bleed
It might've been enough for us
but for all those ghosts to feed

They were only stolen flowers
yet by any other name
I had you until morningfall
beheld you with its flames

dawn joy - October 6, 1975

grey-pearl opalescence in the east,
lighting the hills with ethereal cool.
dawnlight creeps in the window to smile upon us,
lying in dreamy sleep-haze,
a counterpoint of light and dark -
black hair, warm pale-brown skin
mingling with creamy white.
soft voices, softer looks with dark eyes shining.
dawn grows brighter, pale yellow then rose.
warmth and joy grow in the crystalline light.
early mornings
to wake with you beside me,
dawn joy glows in my heart,
our journey - so new, so beautiful.

dawn joy, redux - August 26, 2015

and now, it is morning again.
grey-pearl opalescence
    still glows in the east.
here we are, we two,
    counterpoint of light and dark.
and how many mornings does it take
    to make a marriage?
over fourteen thousand.
it is a number beyond
    the reach of my mind.
at first, I loved you,
    but I knew so little of you,
    and you of me.
and now? I love you with depth
    and breadth and height,
    with the passion of a thousand stars.
fourteen thousand mornings,
    some (most) with love,
    some (few) with ire.
but those storms have passed,
    and still and stronger do we love.
dawn joy is a fire in my heart.
our journey - so long, so beautiful.

GARY DALEN

Timid Romantic

If you're a romantic stay away from everyday real life
because you won't find what you're looking for,
not even a glimmer.
In everyday real life we fall in line;
keeping a safe distance from the dread of humiliation.
We work our minds and starve our hearts
in order to accumulate iconographic kitsch,
labels upon labels for that we stand in line.
If one does not want to experience humiliation and separation; they
must stay in line and forego romanticism.

To be a romantic you must entertain the schizo insane
and open wide those locked doors of perception
where there is neither truth nor lies, good nor evil, right nor wrong.
Where one is naked without disguise;
entering into stardust darkness fully illuminated;
without vulnerability to embarrassment;
where one does not hate thyself or the world they once did despise.

AUDREY MEI

If I am breathing,
    I am thinking of you.
If my eyes are open,
    I am wishing you would appear.
When I speak, the words take flight
    and search to be heard by you.
And every passing second is a waiting time
The virgin sphinx watches the horizon,
    eternal yet so shy
that not even the eroding wind of the centuries
dares whisper this longing for you.

Tongue Swapping 2

I swallowed my tongue
in bedroom shine,
shat it out, swapped it
with my neighbor Elizabeth.

Now Elizabeth romances my GF
Sarah in my voice. Sarah
is down yet peppers out questions:

Does this make me gay?
Can you wear our dildo tonight?
Do you have any lube?

she barks over her black IPA
at a highway bar. They swerve home
past my red robin door.

Transpose through, I rattle
Elizabeth's tongue before her husband.
Elizabeth and William made theirs
official in Las Vegas.

Under lamplight, is this a roadside love?
I search William's suburban eyes
for a sign of life. Yes, I'll cling to this

in my nursing home days.
When I speak in our present groove,
he silences me with a wet kiss.

ANA DELGADILLO

Message from Time to Clock

Time

One day I asked myself as I passed your window.
How is it I move forward yet you stay still
in the corner next to unbuilt cuckoos' nests
that will become the noisy hearts of your brethren?

My movements better caught with
each leaf floating in an autumn breeze,
in the quiet sway of dandelions as their seeds
separate, spread throughout the spring scent
of newborn grass, of daffodils as small yellow
lamps that warm the earth as it rotates.

Each step I take dulled by the tic-toc
of starched splinters in your hands,
in the slow progression of what ifs:
If your tomorrow were just an hour for me.
If your hands were to break how will you hold me
If *if* were now and you were yesterday.

Clock

I saw as you passed my window,
I saw as you stared at me from the warmth
of the summer heat, you passed like dew
along the chill of your temples. Yes I saw
it drip, seconds in my small child's hand.

She held onto you, a balloon, her tiny figure
giggling as you thought her hops too slow.
Her slender form a shadow
to the minute, to her older hour.

But you stopped and stared. Why as time,
you feel I sit here, still, my wooden frame
aging with you like a loyal husband, catching
your memories along with each sway
of my pendulum?

Maybe I'm not as romantic
as the falling of flower petals,
as funny as the hyacinths,
whose laughter fill the emptiness,
the calming scent of gardenias
that tag along, but here I wait.

I always wait, because without me
who will remember that you've come by
to visit? Who else but I can hold you
even when you think you've gone?

ROUND TRIP

LEENA PRASAD

time

hours minutes seconds
tick-tocking the parameters
of my day, my life
time, an enemy, a friend
whispering impermanence

FRANCES HILLYARD

I see you among yellow roses
black plastic bag pulled up over
your jaundiced face
flattened gurney tilted up against the stairs.

It was not a fond farewell. I had
thought I'd get out my dancing shoes. But
there's no dance left in my heart
where love for you lived once.

Shroud my face in black plastic.
Already I have disappeared and this
sad stranger pretending to be me emerged.

DEE DISOMMA

A long and lonely vigil

A long and lonely vigil,
    awaiting a loved one's death.
Alone or with companions,
    loneliness rules the time.

We each are alone with our memories,
    the good times from the past.
We share them with the others,
    but they only live in our hearts.

To watch as bones grow visible,
    presaging the skeleton to come,
As skin grows thinner, like gossamer,
    and drapes around the frame.

To bid farewell over and over,
    as death comes near at hand.
One fears to be silent while waiting
    for the end of earthly love.

A form of death for the living
    to wait and watch like this.
One could water the desert with teardrops
    shed at this loneliest time.

At the end, the dead are peaceful,
    but the living have grief to stay,
An unbidden guest that lingers
    long after the welcome has passed.

PHOENIX GILLIAM

Two Survivors

She threw back the gates of her isolation
and absorbed me
beneath the ages
of earth in her face
to the buried city
where children had played

We spoke of the fall
father's falling bootstraps toward the room
like god and rain falling from the sky
blood and angels falling on the floor
we were ghosts, and ghosts of ghosts
when they were through

Carrying more than we wanted
and less than we needed
on the diaspora of innocents
to the fallen world

The mountains we could not climb
we carried
over other mountains

Gathering new countries around us
of carnival mirror souls
who reflected, not beauty but recognition

"Does it ever come back to you?" she asked.
I said, "It's like being on a train
and looking through the window of the next train
and seeing yourself
and he looks back at you
but the car slowly pulls away
and you watch yourself go."

Lying beside her I thought of Helen Keller
raging in her inarticulation
and how those first words
must have felt like being born

And I wondered if Helen
ever met another like herself
with neither sight nor sound

and what secret language

they must have whispered

into each other's hands

ANA DELGADILLO

Río Papaloapan

I was born in a time when butterflies bloomed
beneath the leaves of a banana tree,
nearby a river flowed to meet the wide Atlantic,
its roots swallowed, embraced,
its sweetness blended with the saltiness
of my mother's sweat as she gave birth to me.

It seems that time tends to mix our lives,
like salt and sugar in a child's hands
when asked to fill the sugar jar.
A father's anger, a mother's laughter
as he sips his coffee before he leaves.

I was born near a river,
but not *el río de mariposas*,
the great *Papaloapan*
that spans its vein through Oaxaca,
with sugar cane as its skin.

A river like any other river, maybe,
but to me it is where my *Abuelo*
used to drive to visit the Cathedral
in Tuxtepec, a family in unison
like the banana trees clustered
so tight a small child can't squeeze through.

Those were the days I remember most,
we were happy, but I was a child
happiness was in the *coco* milk,
in the food, and in my *Abuelo's* laughter,
in watching the river flow through time
and my family with it.

I remember the river,
for I was born in a time when butterflies bloom,
and one bloomed inside of me.

EXPRESS WAYS

AUDREY MEI

orgies of the electrical poets

fingering ourselves before a
virtual one-way Window
we pet, stroke, perspire, and peak
with each other,
strangers in the eNight
swan-diving into an electrical sea
with our hearts lanced open
arteries erupting in
arcs and streams of
words

                    and we are caught
                    by a net of cyber hands
                    tickling our hungry
                    and emoting skins
                    from myriad keyboards
                    across the Qwerty
                    world, the deepest
                    penetration into the
                    smoldering web which
                    exudes and drips and
                    squeezes and spoils
                    the Ink,
                    drying on the page
                    crystallized
                    into kilobytes of
                    Verse.

We all sing together
the anthem of the ePoet
as we snap another digital
self-pic from arm's length
and Save one another
on a lonely Saturday night
and gushing
we profess
love
to us
kindred
electric souls.

GARY DALEN

Recipe for a painter

Everybody goes through hell
don't they?
Questions, answers,
body feelings of pain,
shaking nerves, inverted orgasms,
cold chilled, guilt fevers, on the
edge of life, true contemplation
of death to end seizures of chills
that run up and down the back and
around the shoulders.
I will endure the nauseation
and breathe pollution one more day.
All I need is the privacy of three walls.
Endless supply of rice and
red wine.
One paint brush,
three colors,
and a piece of canvas.
Be able to kiss and hug my
two boys at least once a day.
And an occasional date with a
topless dancer.

unpoetic

words stuck
inside my mind's maze
refusing access
today I've lost my poet's soul
today I cannot be myself

the soft hiss of pencil on paper

paper,
> white, blank, empty;
> a potentiality
> waiting for fulfillment.

pencil,
> graphite grey,
> another possibility
> ready to create.

straightedge, compass, eraser:

with all these tools,
> unlimited ideas
> can grow into realities.

the rhythm of
> line on paper;
> the pause for thought
> while creativity brews.

erasing one idea,
> blending with another.;
> the image stirs the mind
> into new dimensions.

quiet work;
> nothing disturbs
> the soft hiss of
> pencil on paper.

what comes of this?
> a garment?
> a house?
> a poem.

THE POETS

Gary Dalen is a San Francisco poet who has been writing poems, prose, & lyrics for over four decades. He writes with sincerity and honesty usually never editing or rewriting his poems. His poems are a by product of existential tormentation with a dash of springtime hope, visions of inaccessible light, reminiscent of the never ending task of avoiding the never ending now.

Ana Delgadillo was born in Mexico to an American father and Mexican mother and currently teaches high school Spanish. She completed her M.F.A. in creative writing at U. C. Riverside and her works have been published by the Greenhouse Review and appeared in Palabra Publications, Border Senses Literary Journal, and Freshwater Literary Journal, among many others. In her writing she draws inspiration from her life in Mexico, growing up in a dual-culture household and from the experience of dealing with depression. Her influences include Cesar Vallejo, Wislawa Symborska, Mary Oliver, Phillip Levin and more.

Dee diSomma was born in New York City and grew up on Long Island with strong connections to her maternal ancestors who settled the East End. She studied geology in college but always wrote as a means of expression. She moved to the Bay Area for graduate school and has lived in Northern California ever since. However, she was, is, and always will be a New Yorker; you can't change her birth certificate.

Keith Mark Gaboury earned a M.F.A. in creative writing from Emerson College, but then he needed to move from fantasy to money. So he started working as a preschool teacher. In 2016, Keith rode a dragon from Massachusetts to California, her claws now planted in Oakland. He now writes poetry and instills dragon empathy into young minds. Learn more at: keithmgaboury.com.

Phoenix Gilliam is a seeker and survivor who has haunted hidden places in Berkeley and the greater Bay Area all his life. When he's not writing or reading he can usually be found climbing and sculpting trees, or looking for new adventures on his motorcycle.

Frances Hillyard has used poetry to serve both contemplation and activism. Her inspiration comes from art, music, nature, personal philosophy, and experience. She was recently the Poet Laureate of the Berkeley Fellowship of Unitarian Universalists.

Audrey Mei graduated in cello performance from New England Conservatory of Music and with a degree in biological psychology from Tufts University. She received a Fulbright Grant to for cello at Sibelius Academy in Helsinki, Finland. Her writing has been published by Burning Cities Press, Glimmer Train, Gangway Literary Magazine, Haunted Waters Press, and many more. Her novel, *Trixi Pudong and the Greater World*, was a finalist for the 2016 Foreward Reviews Award for Multicultural Fiction.

Leena Prasad, M.A., Stanford University, has authored two books: *iT felt Like A kiss*, an exploration of art in the Mission district of San Francisco, and *not exactly haiku*, a collection of short poems. She founded and published *Accent*, a South-Asian literary magazine. Leena published a story about her father in the anthology *Untold Stories: From the Deep Part of the Well* and a poem in *Sonoma: Stories of a Region and Its People*. She has also written for *The Press Democrat, India Currents, Mission Arts Monthly, KQED Spark*, and various other media outlets. In her other life, she is a software executive. Portfolio at www.FishRidingABike.com.

Kazue Watanabe is originally from Japan. She has lived in San Francisco since 2005 and works in an online education company as a test engineer. She spends her spare time reading, writing poems and essays, which are usually based on her experience living in the SF Bay Area.

Doug Young is a research writer whose research paper "How to Master the Local Bypass Challenge" sold over 20,000 copies in the B2B telecom market. He has a master's degree from Harvard and studied fiction writing with Peter Taylor at the University of Virginia. His work has been published in Paragon Journal. Doug attended ThrillerFest and the Book Passage Mystery Writers Conference. His hobbies include rowing on the San Francisco Bay.

www.ingramcontent.com/pod-product-compliance
Lightning Source LLC
Chambersburg PA
CBHW071252070526
44583CB00017B/2437